"When I'm mad, my face gets tight and my body gets hot and I want to punch my sister. My mom says I can't do that though."
Connor - age 5

"This book is amazing! It teaches applied principles of meditation and mindfulness all wrapped up in a fun story kids will love. Great book!"

 Dr. Clarita Margarido, Physician, Professor, Researcher

"Few children's books really focus on children's emotions and actually help them regulate them in a healthy way without adult intervention. As a high school teacher, I see countless students today struggling to cope with their anger and various emotions. Wellness and teaching resilience should be at the top of parents' and teachers' priority lists when it comes to caring for children. I pray that as children step through the hard circumstances of life, they read this book with a parent (or in a classroom), and learn that there are many healthy ways to release our anger instead of hurting others and ourselves. Kudos on another excellent book Colleen Aynn."

 Rachel Nazareth, MDiv, OCT TCDSB Secondary Educator

"Wonderful! Knowing how to deal with your feelings is inspiring and **Mad Michael** teaches us the importance of listening to our feelings, especially as children! Great lessons are paired with beautiful illustrations throughout the book, making the reading experience so enjoyable. Highly recommend for kids, adults & educators alike."

 Dr. Monica Eloy, Physician, Consultant

"This book is amazing! It teaches kids to regulate their emotions in ways that that work for them. It is important to remind kids that we are all different and need help to overcome our own obstacles. Strategies for self-regulation and mindfulness in a fun story for little kids. Well done!"

 Vince Chininea, Principal HCDSB

Published by Hasmark Publishing
http://www.hasmarkpublishing.com

Copyright© 2017 by Colleen Aynn
First Edition, 2017

No part of this book may be reproduced or transmitted in any form or by any means, electronic or mechanical, including photocopying, recording or by any information storage and retrieval system, without written permission from the author, except for the inclusion of brief quotations in a review.

Disclaimer

This book is designed to provide entertainment to readers and is sold purely for entertainment purposes. This is a work of fiction. Characters, names, places, events, incidents and circumstances are a product of the author's imagination and are used fictitiously. Any resemblance to actual persons, living or dead, business establishments, companies or locales is entirely coincidental and is not intended by the author.

The publisher does not have control over and does not assume responsibility for the author or third party websites. Neither the publisher nor the individual author(s) shall be liable for any physical, psychological, emotional, financial, or commercial damages, including, but not limited to special, incidental, consequential, or other damages.

Permission should be addressed in writing to Colleen Aynn at feelingfriendsfeedback@gmail.com

Illustrator: Matrix Media Solutions (P) Ltd.
www.matrixnmedia.com

Cover Designer: Colleen Aynn

Layout: Anne Karklins
annekarklins@gmail.com

ISBN-13: 978-1-988071-55-8
ISBN-10: 1988071550

MAD MICHAEL

by
Colleen Aynn

Introduction

Anger was my go to emotion as a kid.

When I couldn't do something... When I didn't get my way... When people did things I didn't like... Pretty much anything, really.

I didn't know how to handle that big feeling inside of me, so I threw up my hands in frustration, yelled, got pissed off, said mean things... I pretty much ran the gamut of bad behaviours when I was angry (as I'm sure all my siblings will attest to).

I had no insight, no idea what to do each time anger showed up on my doorstep, and I certainly never thought about listening to it.

To think that my anger had shown up for a reason, that it was there to tell me something, never entered my mind. Who had ever heard of that???

My parents said all the regular things: "Cut it out! Stop it! Be quiet! Let it go!"

The only problem being, I was then left to my own devices to deal with this giant emotion I didn't know how to handle.

They, like me, had no idea what to do.

Many years of deep work later, I learned that anger was my way of standing up for myself. My yelling was my way of protecting myself when I felt disrespected – not really my best technique, but that's what I knew how to do.

I spent time learning about boundaries, how to figure out what mine were, and then implement them in my life, how to hold them strongly and with integrity and let go of the 'defend or be crushed' mentality I'd always had.

We tend to get nervous around anger. We either submit to the feeling and let it overtake us, or we push it far, far away for fear that it just might.

Makes sense – most people do not know how to deal with their anger, so most of us have only seen bad behaviour around it.

But instead of reacting to the feeling, if we take a second to listen to it, what is our anger telling us? What could our child's anger be saying?

When we look at emotions as messengers from our body, we see a brilliant guidance system, there to point the way and help us figure out what to do next.

"You mean, there's a reason I'm feeling this way??? I'm not nuts??? It's ok???"

Ahhhh! What a relief! I had spent most of my childhood going back and forth from sickly sweet to raging maniac with nothing in between.

Today I'm here to tell you: No, you're not a jerk! No, your child is not crazy! Yes, there's a reason you're feeling this way.

Your anger is here to tell you something.

Have a listen.

C xo

For my brother, Mike.

No, this isn't based on you ;)
It's much more a reflection of who I was growing up.
Thanks for being there & loving me through it.

C xo

It reached up the mountains and rattled the trees.

"Thanks!" said Michael, "You've been such a big help."

"No prob!" said the dog, "Go enjoy yourself!"

Off Michael went, feeling light as a breeze.
No one had ever seen him at ease.

He skipped down the sidewalk, he sailed into school.
Who could believe his calm and his cool?

Now when Michael gets angry, he knows what to do.
He closes his door and lets out his gloom.
He kicks balls in soccer and hits them in tennis,
no longer threatening the town like a menace.

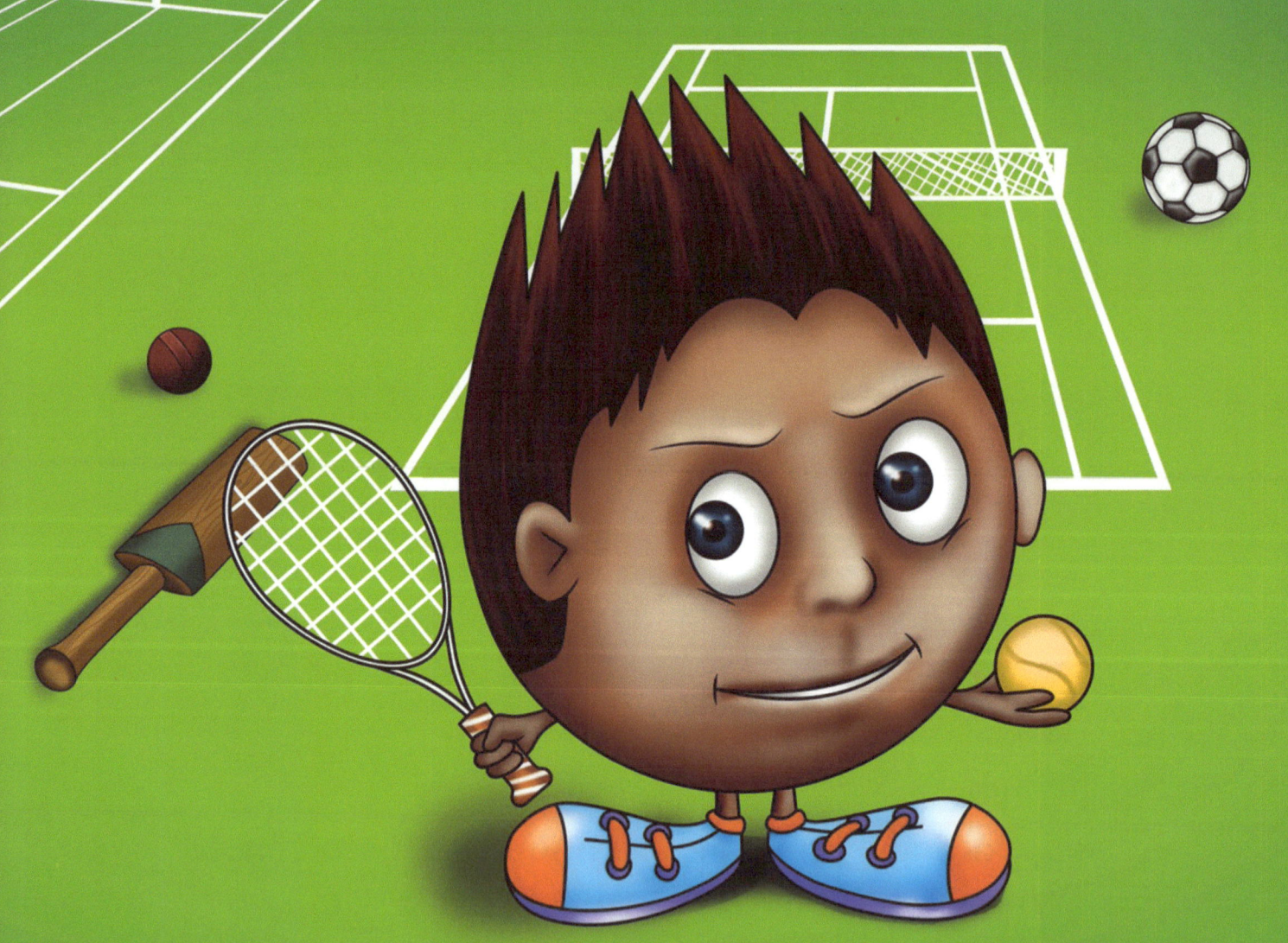

"When I get out my anger, it makes me feel good. I feel calm and relaxed. I feel understood."

About the Author

Colleen is the #1 International Bestselling Author of *Sad Sally*, the first of the Feeling Friends. Having experienced firsthand the healing power of expression, she designed the *Feeling Friends* series to empower children and adults to deal with and express their emotions in positive, healthy ways.

Colleen is also a Professional Speaker Coach & Creator of The EPIC System. For over 30 years she spent her life on stages around the globe as a Professional Actress, Singer and Director. Colleen has now taken this knowledge and experience and broken it down into easy, implementable steps, inspiring people to boldly express themselves and bring their unique voices to the world. Her interactive workshops and online courses teach others how to communicate their message with influence and confidence both on stage and in front of the camera. Come on over to colleenaynn.com and say hi!

Colleen still loves to get up on stage and belt out a tune, and these days she's most often joined by her awesome husband, Bruno and little firecracker, Emilia. Colleen lives in Burlington, Ontario.

"Feeling Friends"

are excited to introduce you to their new friends

The Literary Fairies

TLF is a cool place where you can find out
how YOU could become a published author or
how to help grant a literary wish.
Have an adult visit TLF website for more details about
what we do and how you can help, and also get your
FREE colouring pages and "fill-in-the-blank story"

http://theliteraryfairies.com/free-for-kids/

Join *Sad Sally*, *Mad Michael*, *Nervous Nelly*
and *Happy Hannah* and all their friends as they
navigate through big, emotional days
with the help of some wise animal friends.

Feeling Friends help parents and kids alike, deal with and
express their feelings in constructive, healthy ways.

For more tools, tips and tricks
or to order this magnificent series
visit
feelingfriendsbooks.com
for your BONUS gifts today!

Sad Sally

Happy Hannah

Nervous Nelly

Mad Michael

www.ingramcontent.com/pod-product-compliance
Lightning Source LLC
Chambersburg PA
CBHW041537040426
42446CB00002B/127